EASY COLORING BOOKS
Flowers

Simple Coloring Designs For Rest & Relaxation
by Marta Goertzen

Selah Press

NORTH BEND, OREGON

Marta Goertzen
Selah Press
P.O. Box 1021
North Bend, OR 97459
www.SelahPress.com

Easy Coloring Book: Flowers - Simple Coloring Designs
ISBN 9781703497915

Cover Design: Marta Goertzen

Coloring Designs created with licensed tools from Everdrifter/Drifter Studio

Easy Coloring Books:
Simple Coloring Designs For Rest & Relaxation

Give me a blank journaling page, and it will soon be filled with words and probably a few doodles. Hand me a camera, and I'll quickly fill the memory card with hundreds of photos. Ask me to draw anything more than a stick figure, and you will end up with a collection of scribbles that you will leave you scratching your head.

But I do love to color, and I can prove it with my coloring book, pen, and colored pencil collection. :)

The problem I have encountered with many of the coloring books I've seen and collected is that while beautiful, they are so complicated. The details can be so intricate that a) I need a magnifying glass to see where to color, and b) they take hours to complete. That is not relaxing to me and, I know I can't sit still that long!

Sit Back & Relax:

When I sit down to relax, I like to pull out a simple and easy coloring book with designs that can be completed in a short block of time. Finding coloring books that fit the bill have been hard to find. So I decided to create my own.

Coloring has been shown to help improve focus, reduce stress, and have calming effects on the brain. With this in mind, the coloring designs in this book are intentionally simple and less intricate than many of the coloring books you find at the craft store or online.

Each page is simple enough that you won't need a magnifying glass to color all the small details and easy enough that it won't take days to complete

The designs in this coloring book are intended to be quick and easy. They not necessarily meant to be fine art or frameable art... but of course, frame it if it turns out great! :)

So, sit back, pull out your favorite crayons, markers, or colored pencils, relax and enjoy!

A Few Tips to Keep in Mind:

1) Colored Pencils: Keep the pencil tips sharpened for best coloring.

2) Markers & Pens: Depending on the brand and how hard your press, markers can bleed, if using markers, add an extra sheet behind the design you are coloring.

3) Start Light: You can always color darker, but you can't go from darker to lighter!

4) Relax & Enjoy: Don't stress. Don't be a perfectionist. It's okay to color outside the lines. Relax. Enjoy!

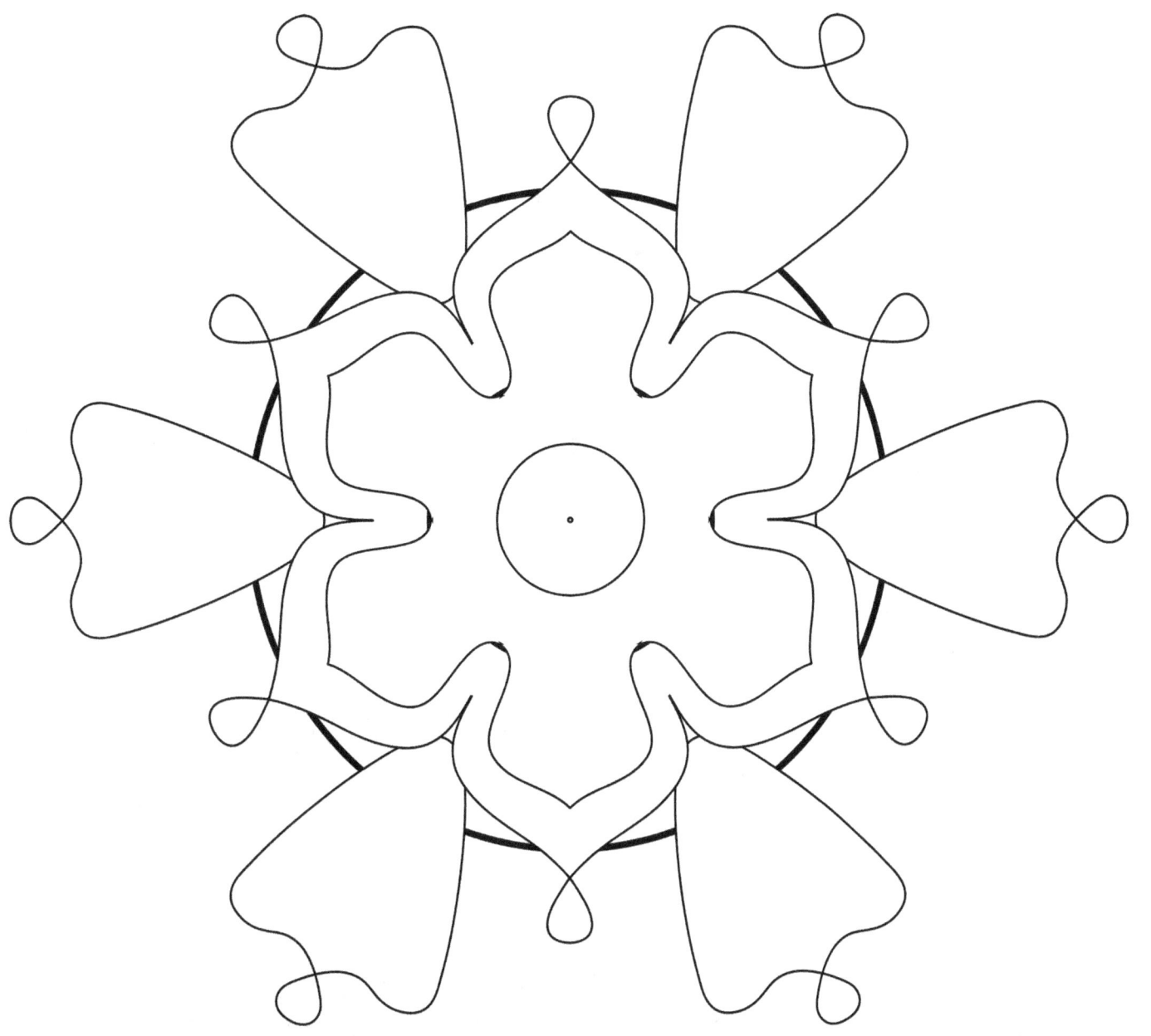

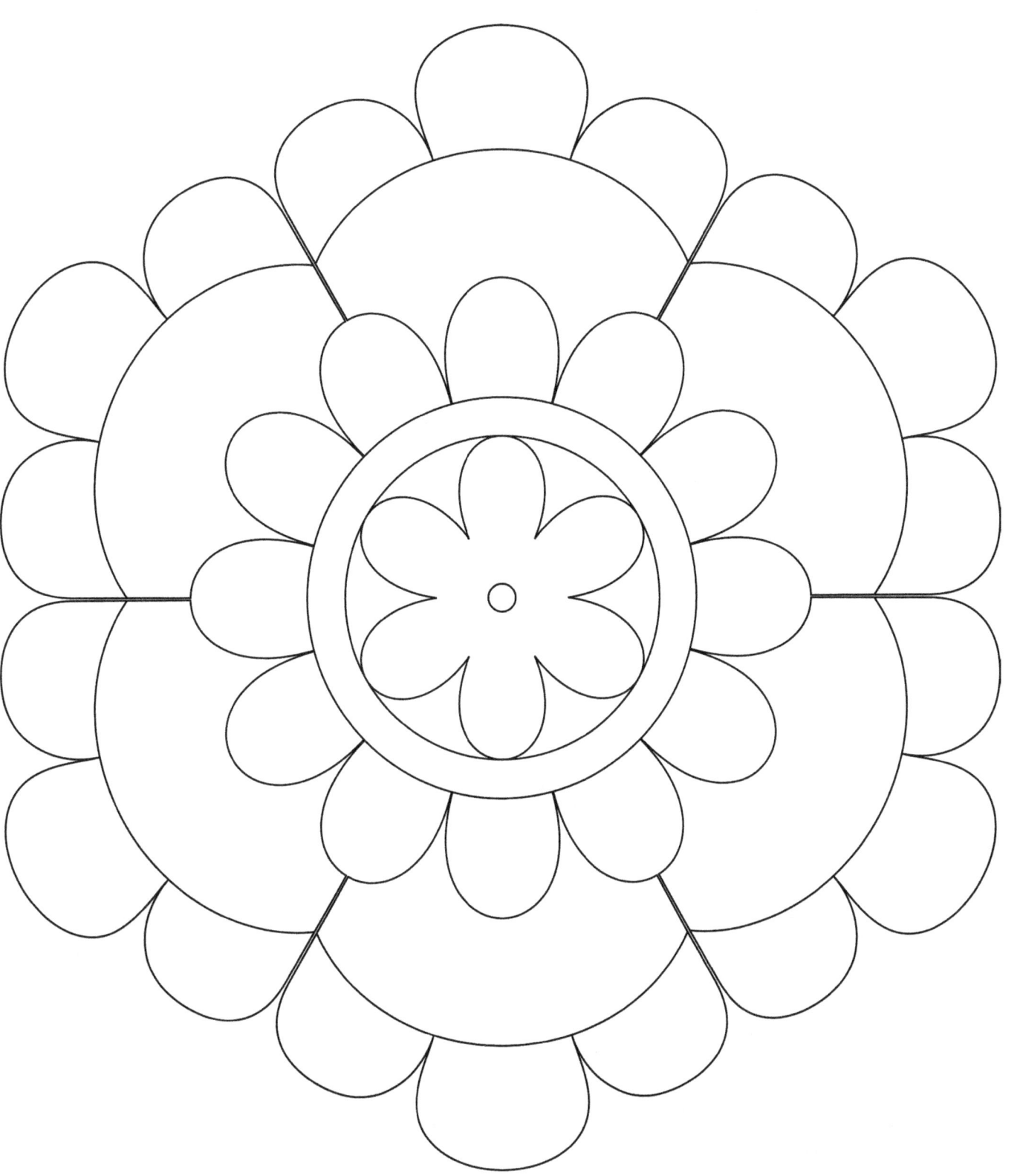

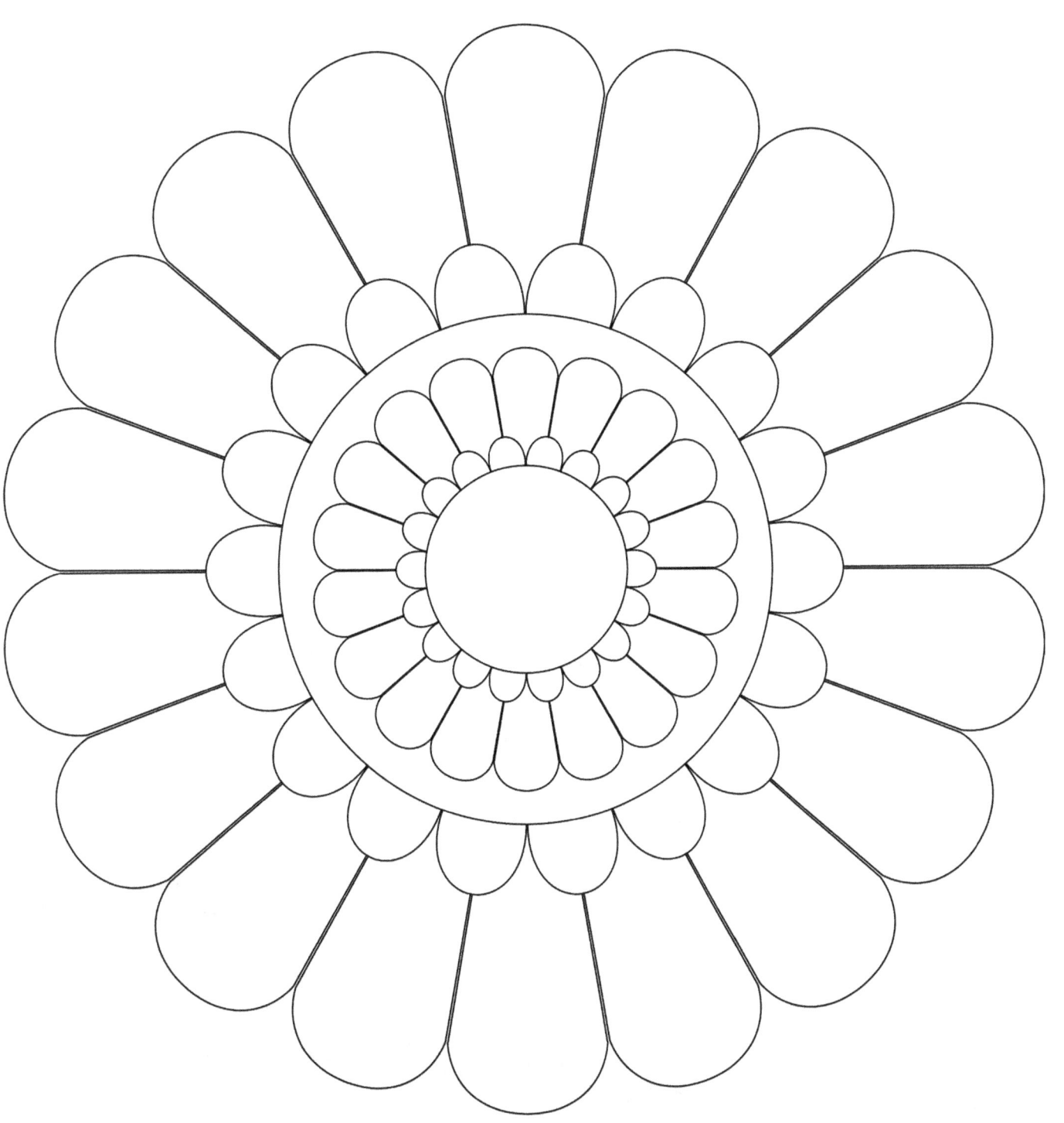

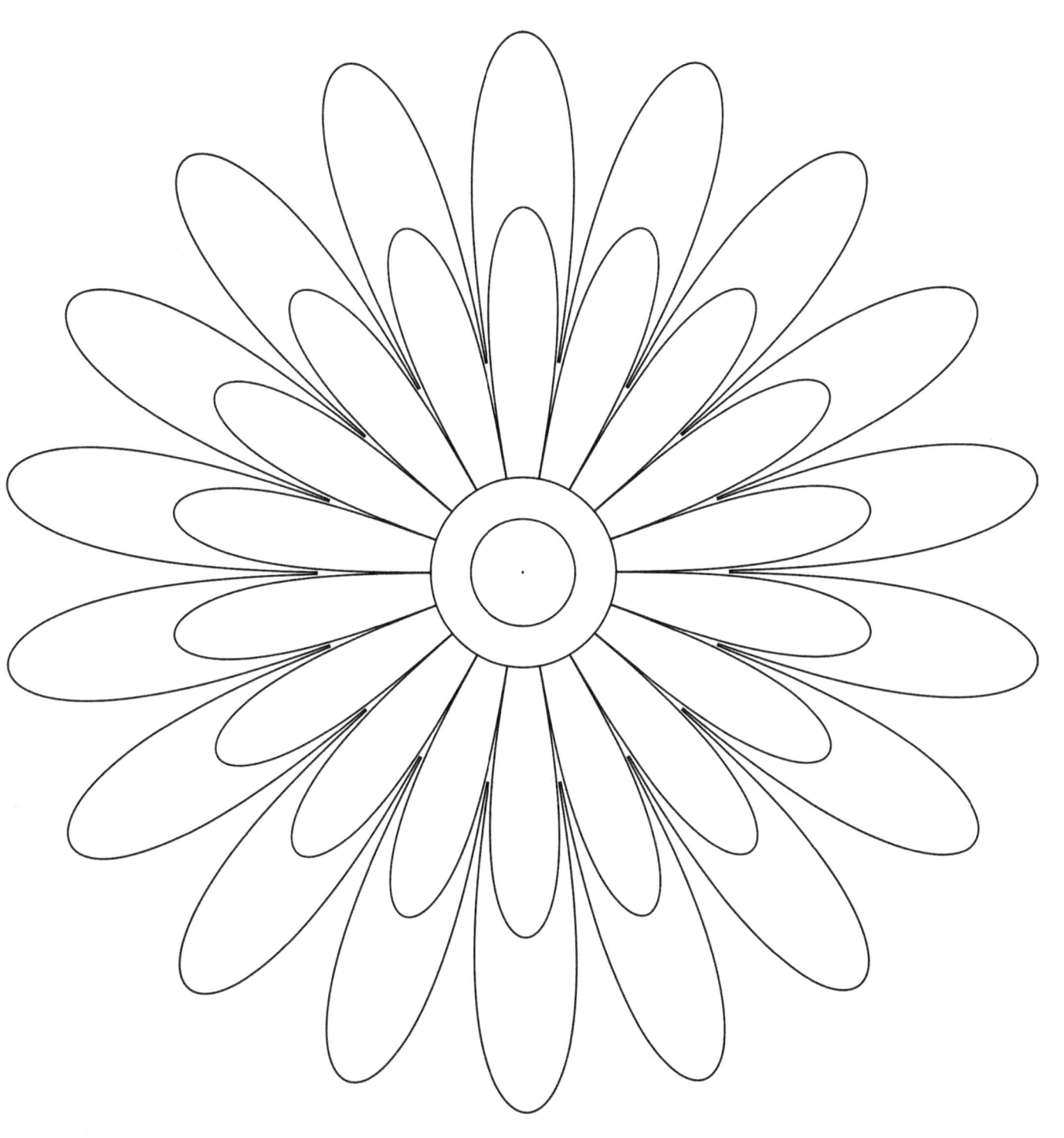

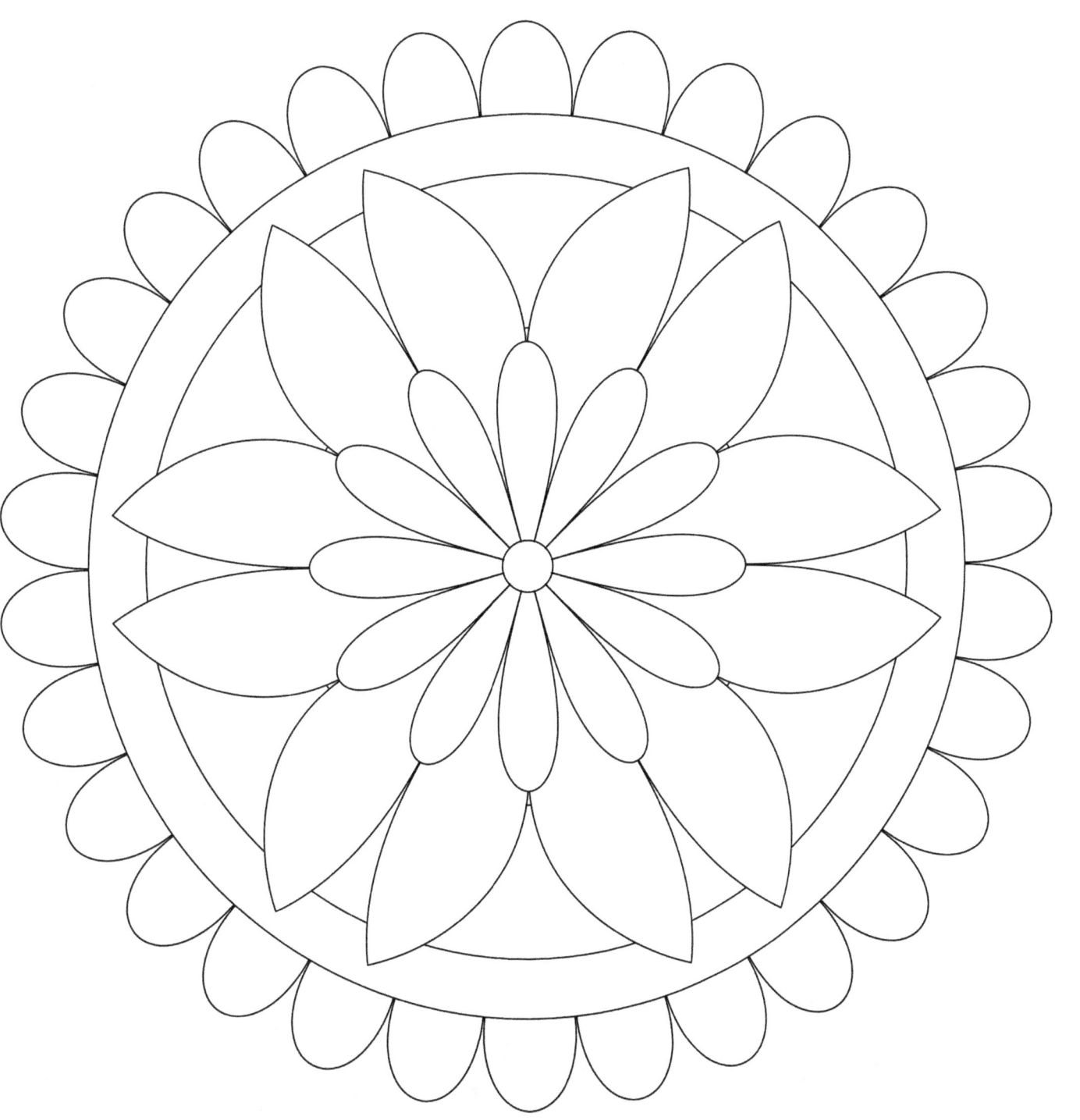

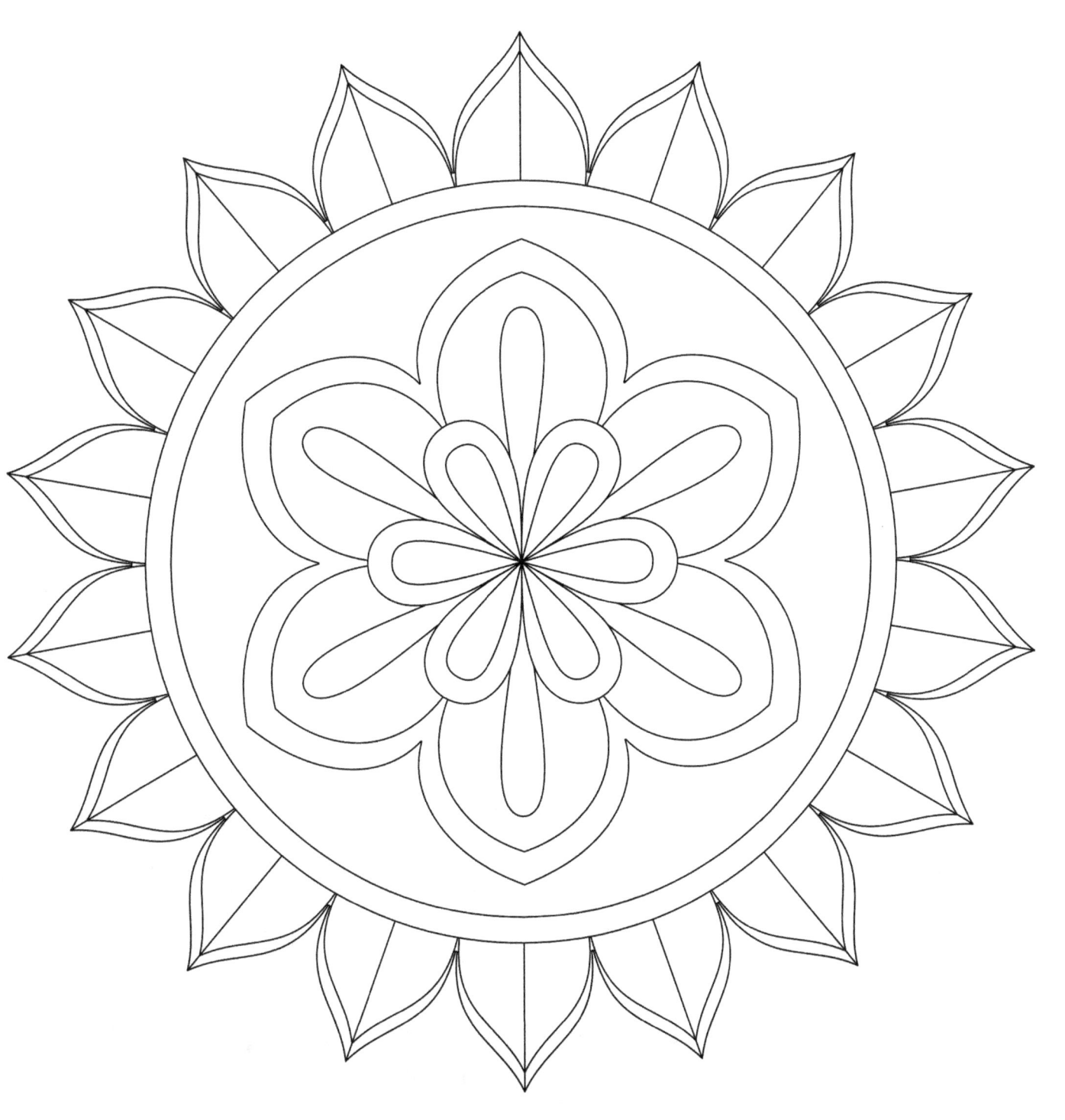

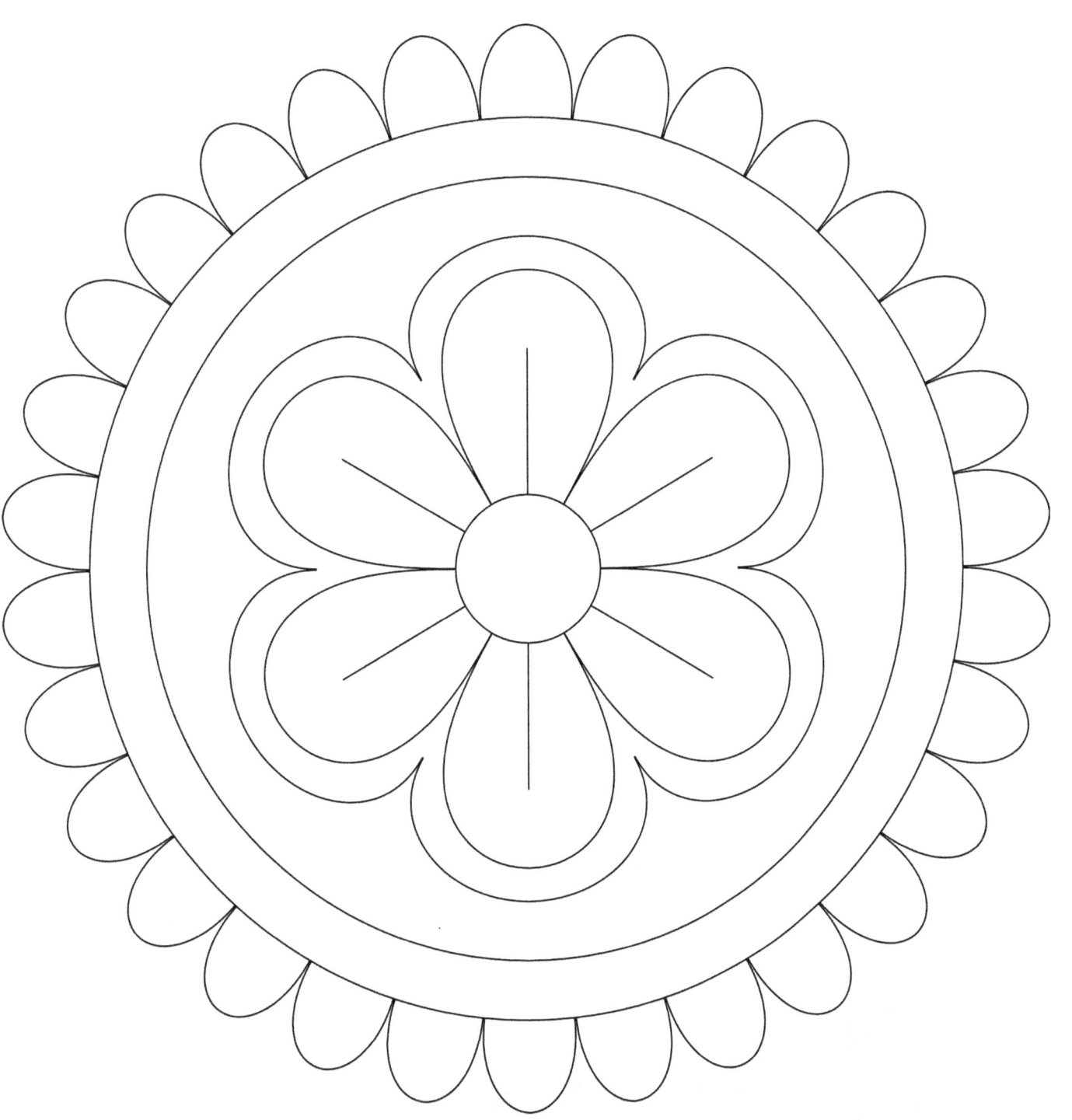

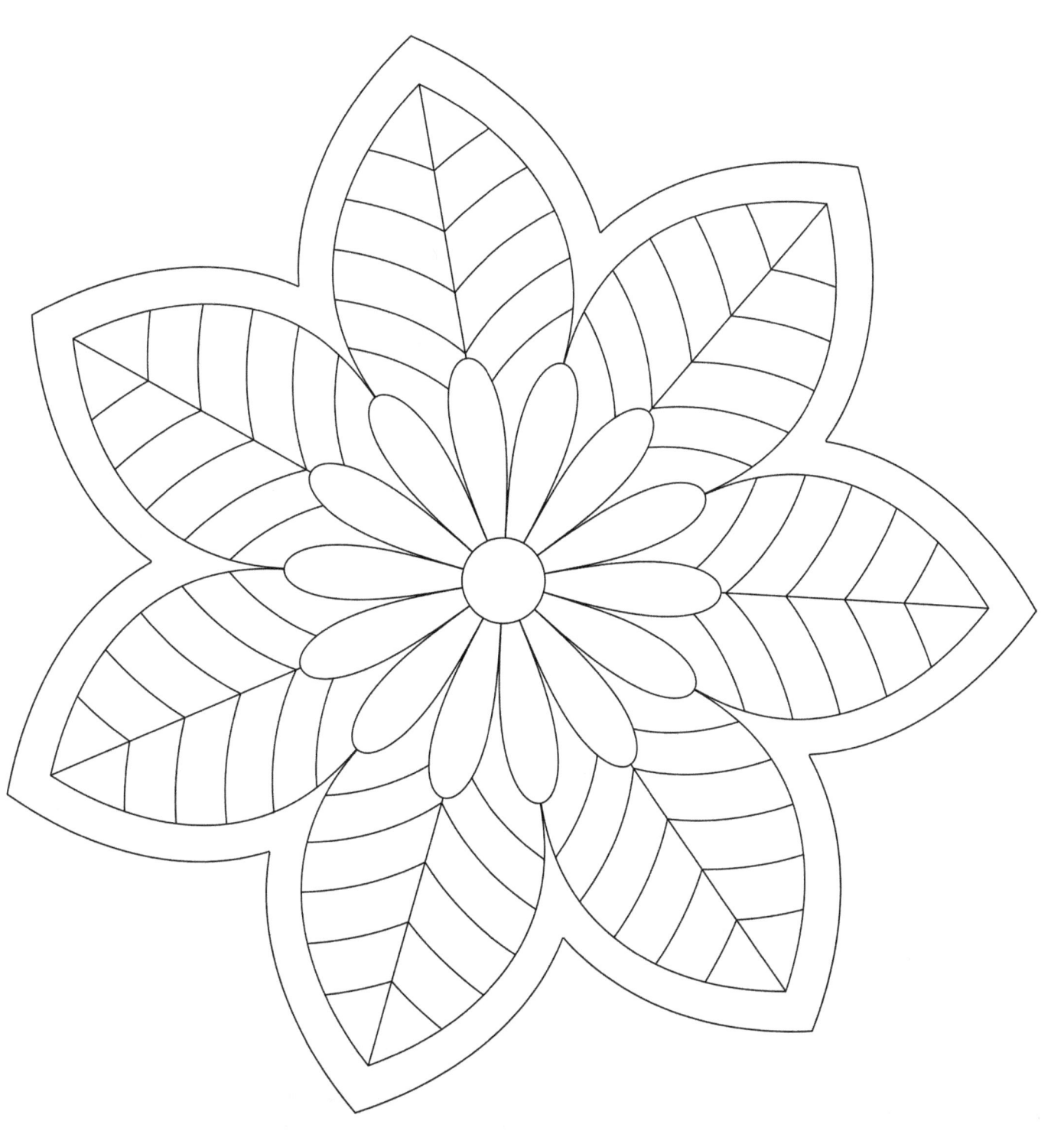

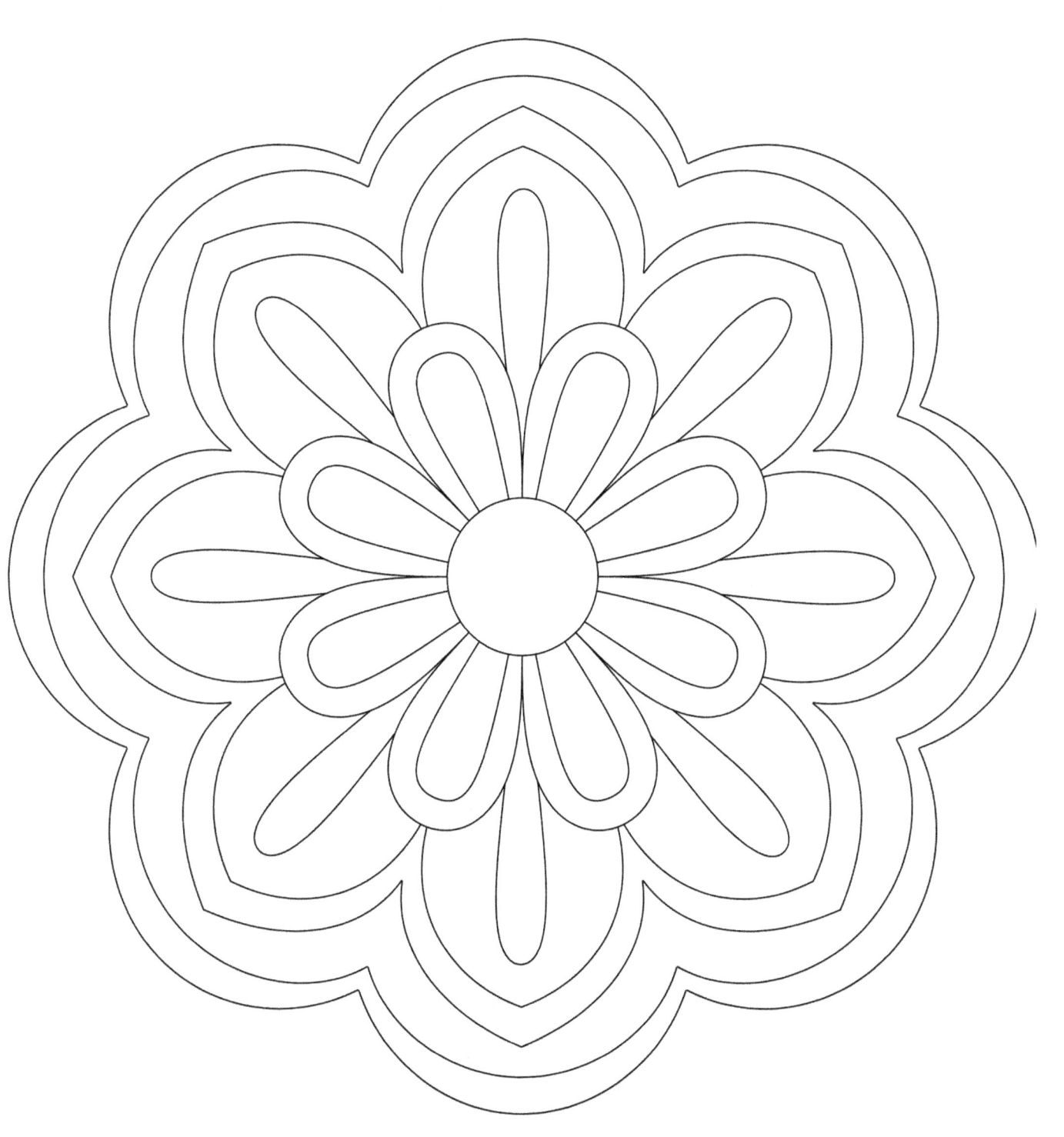

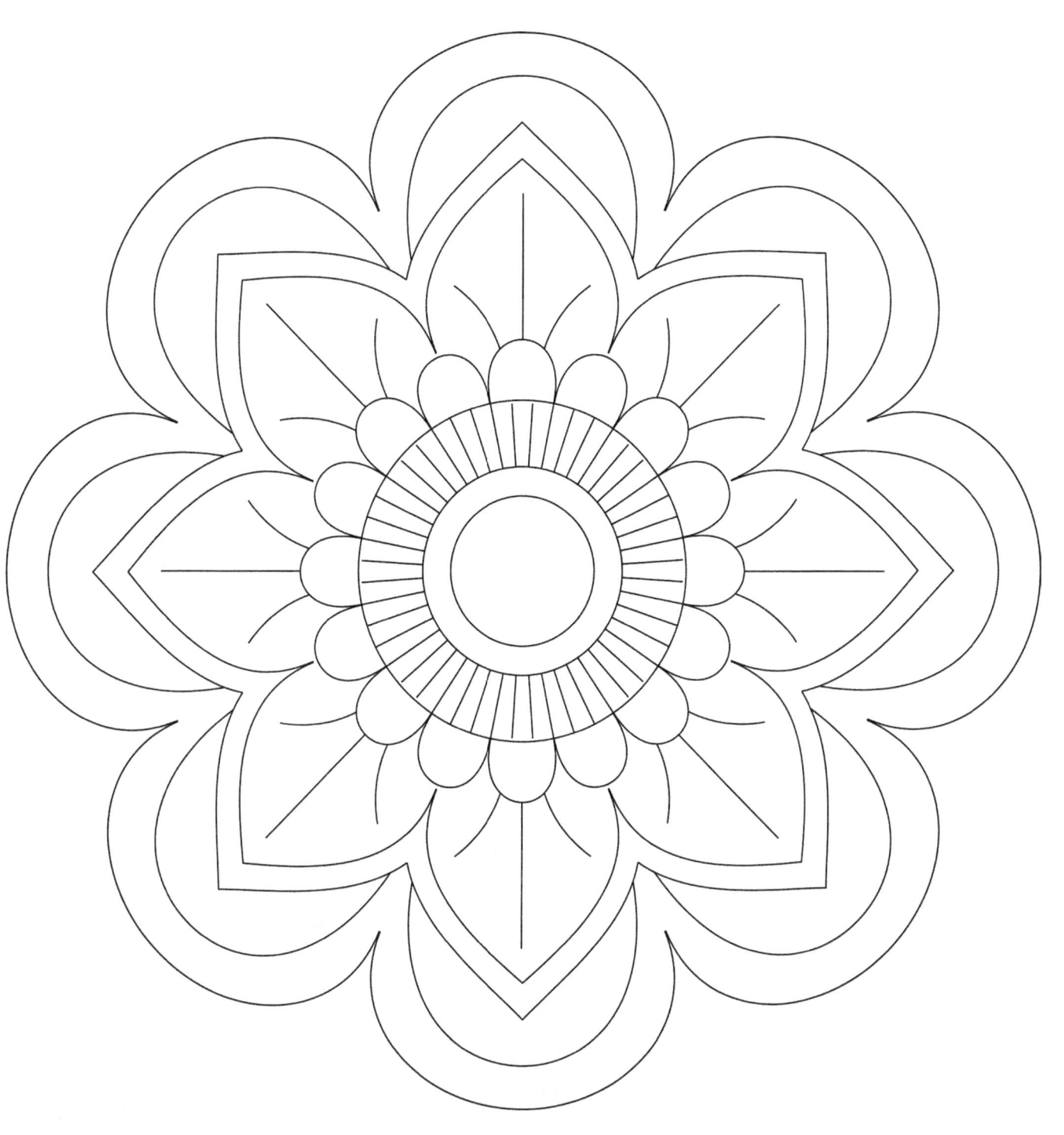

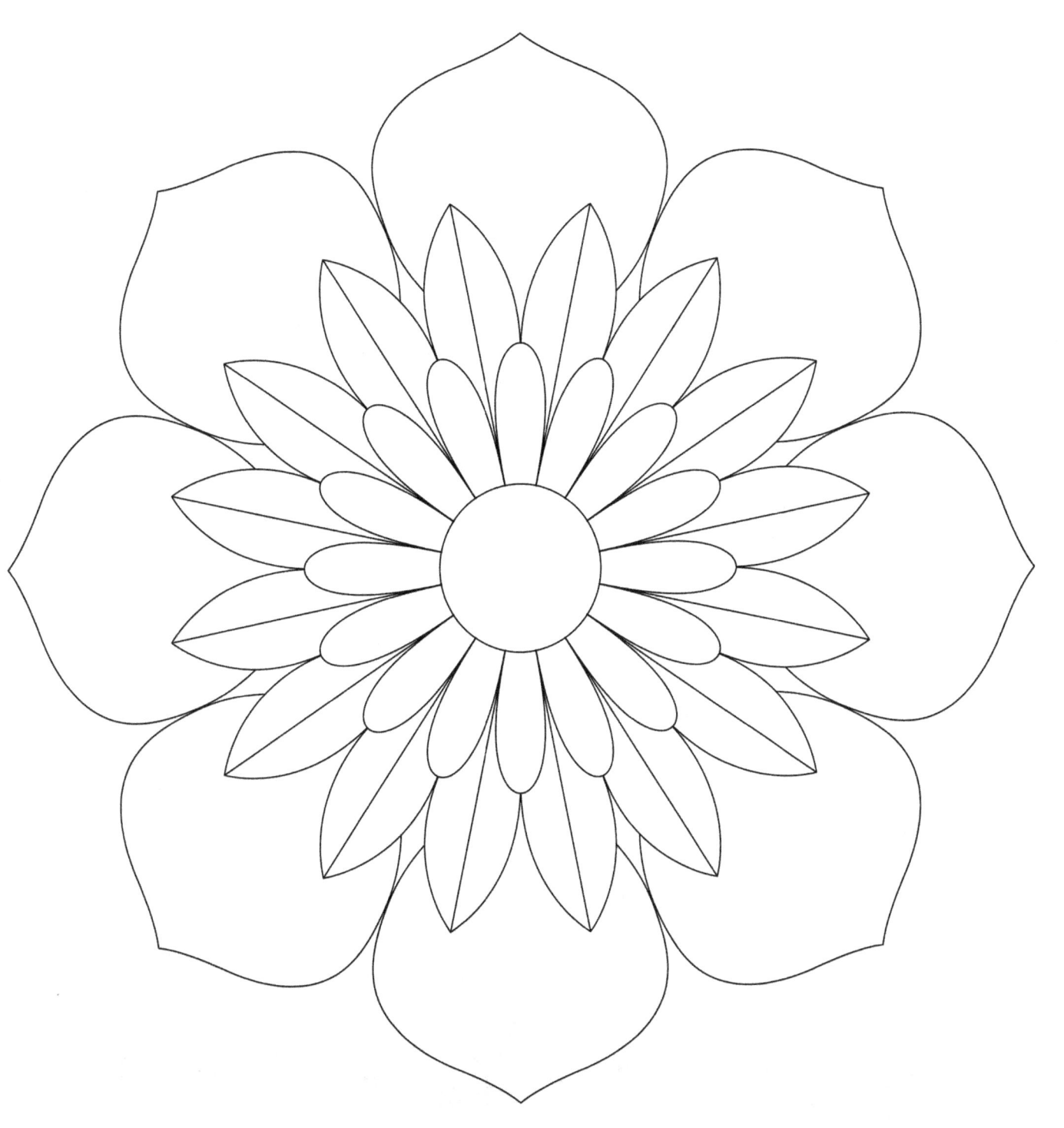

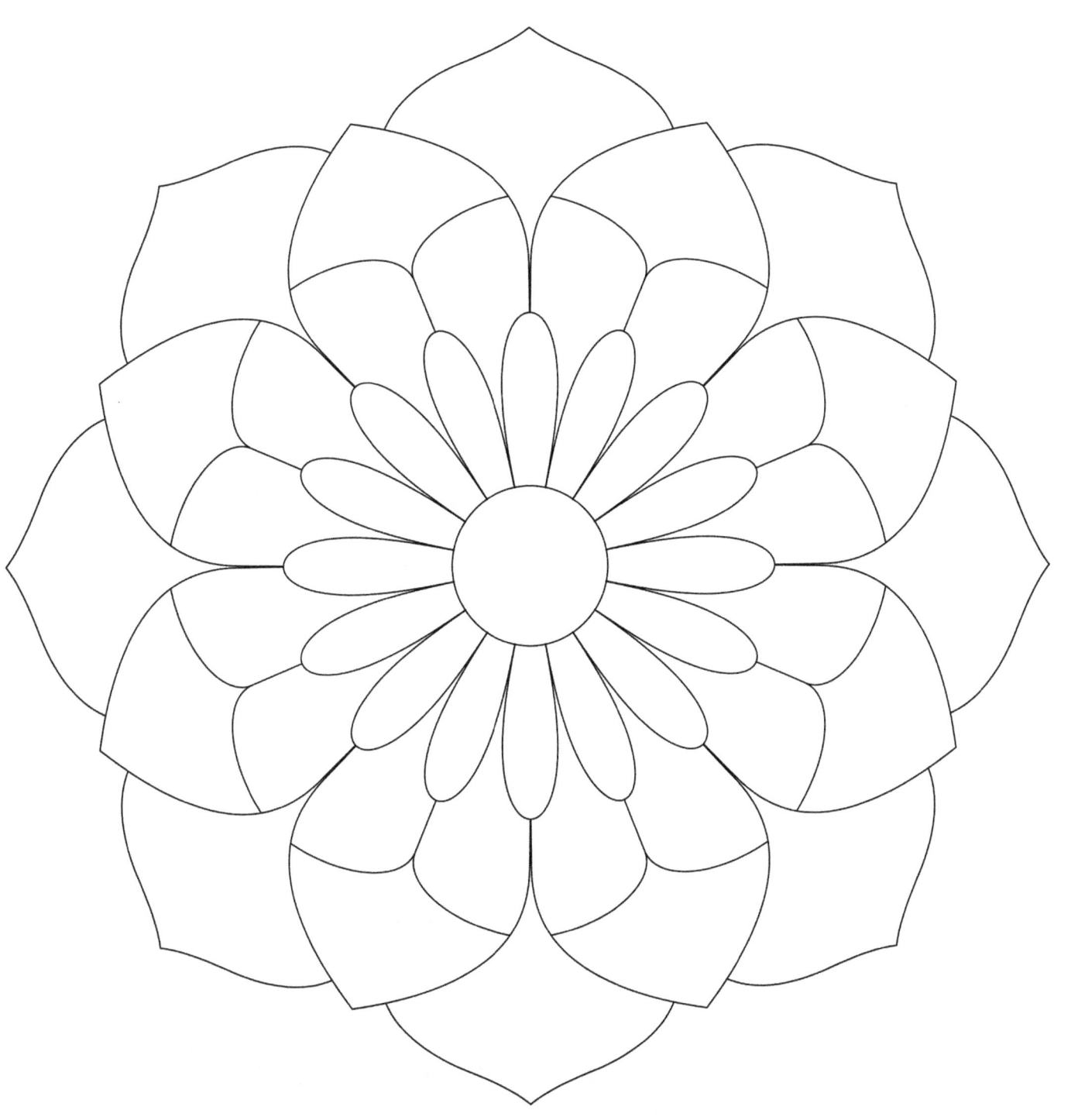

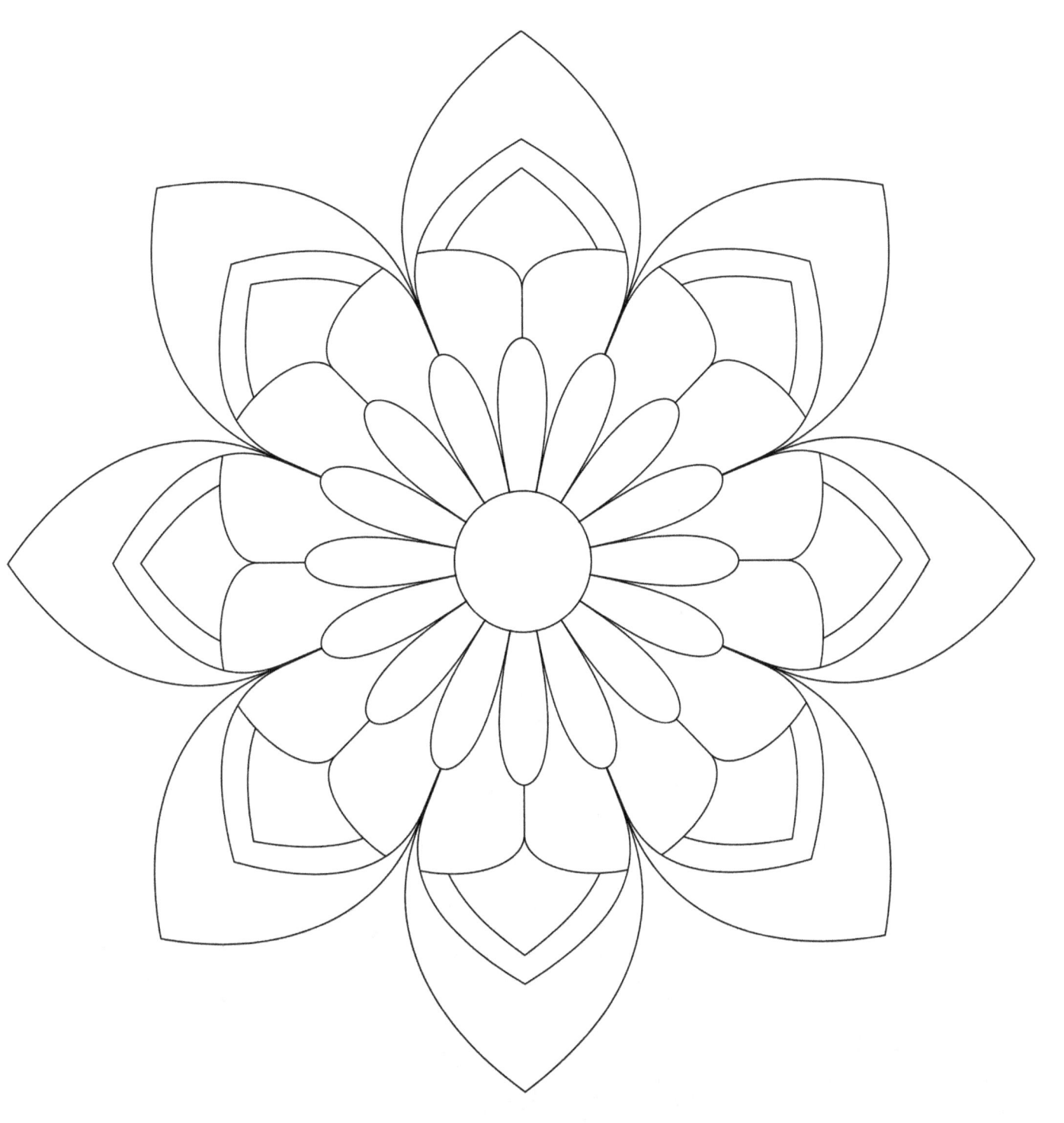

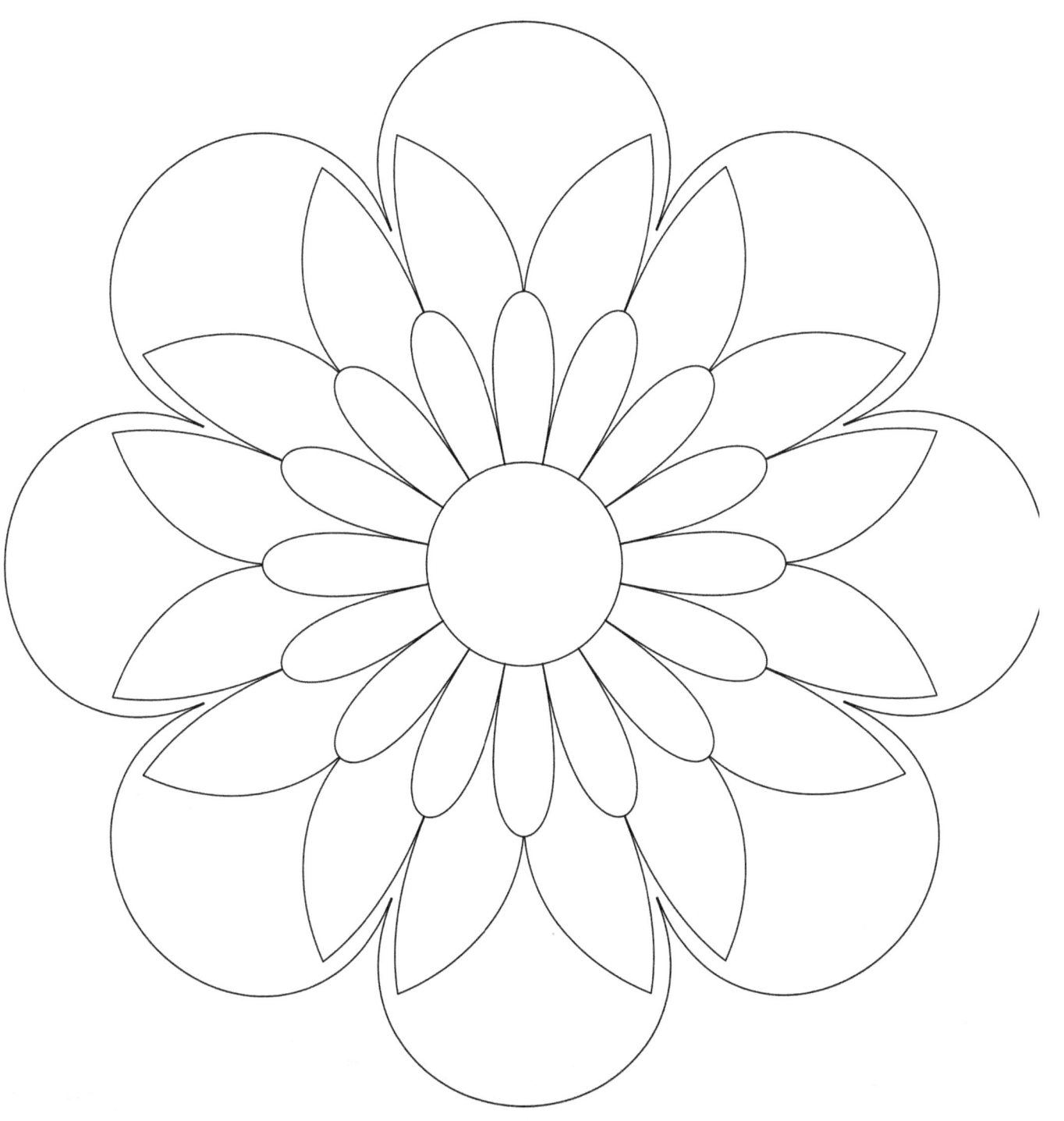

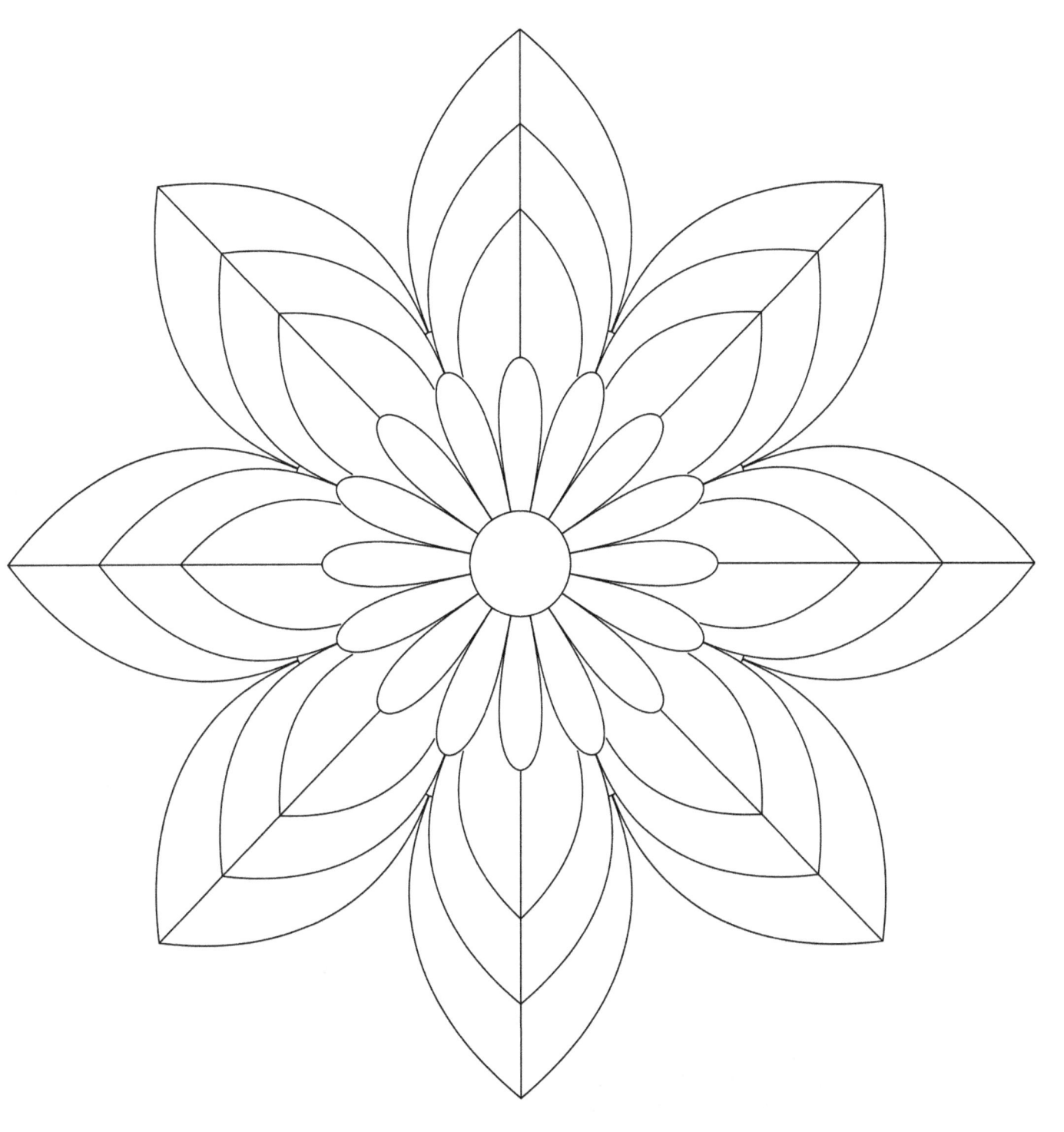

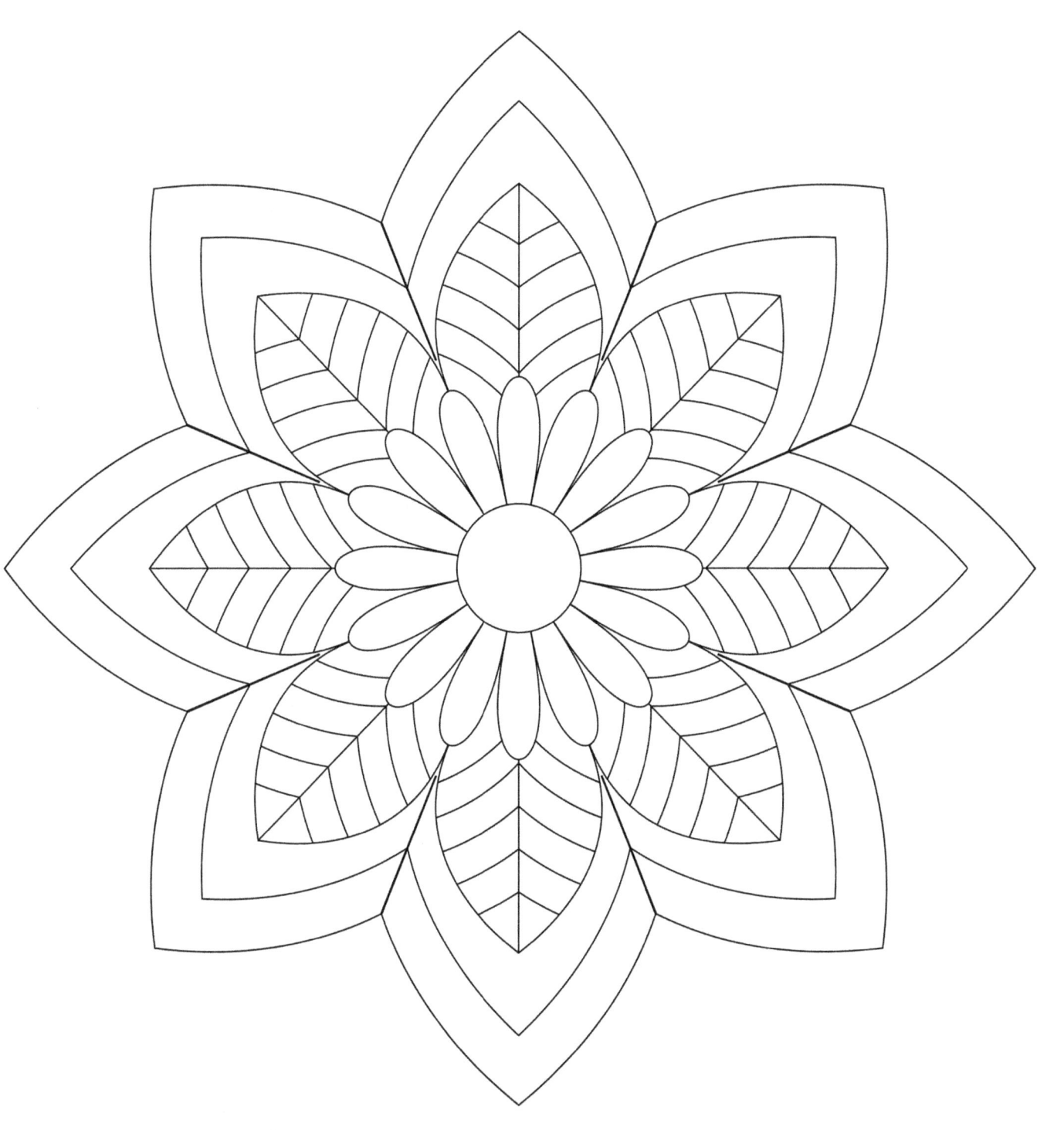

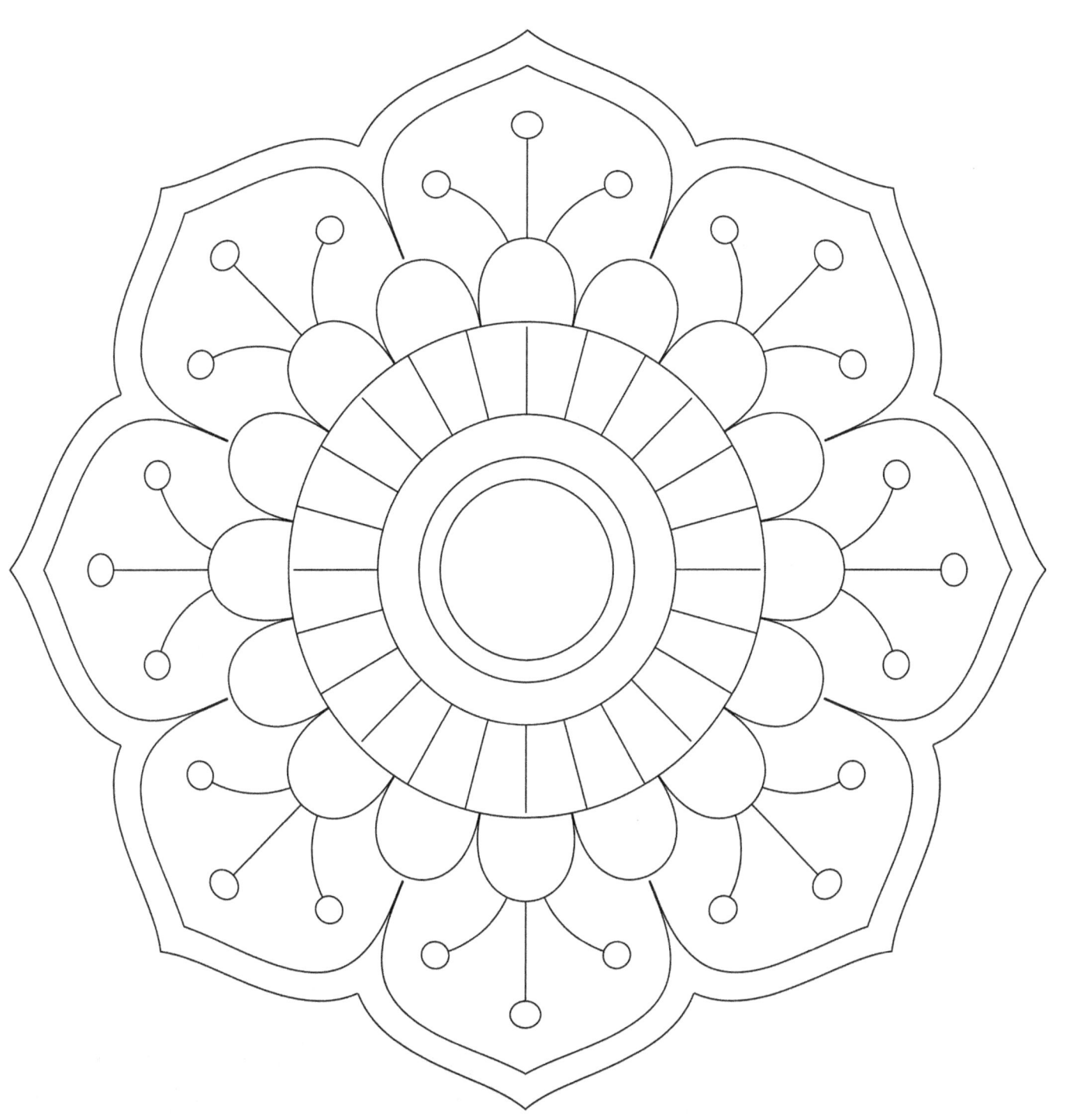

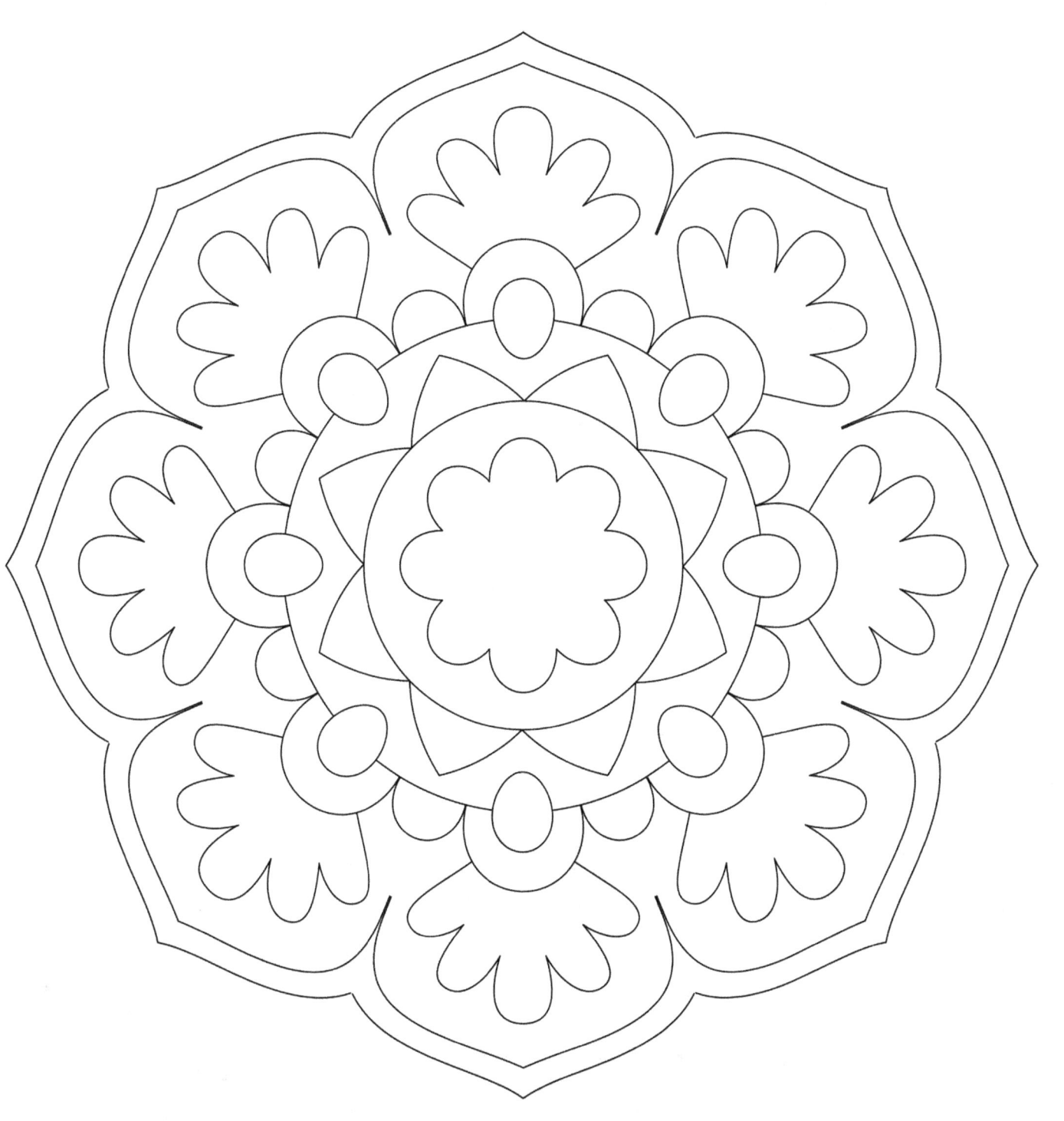

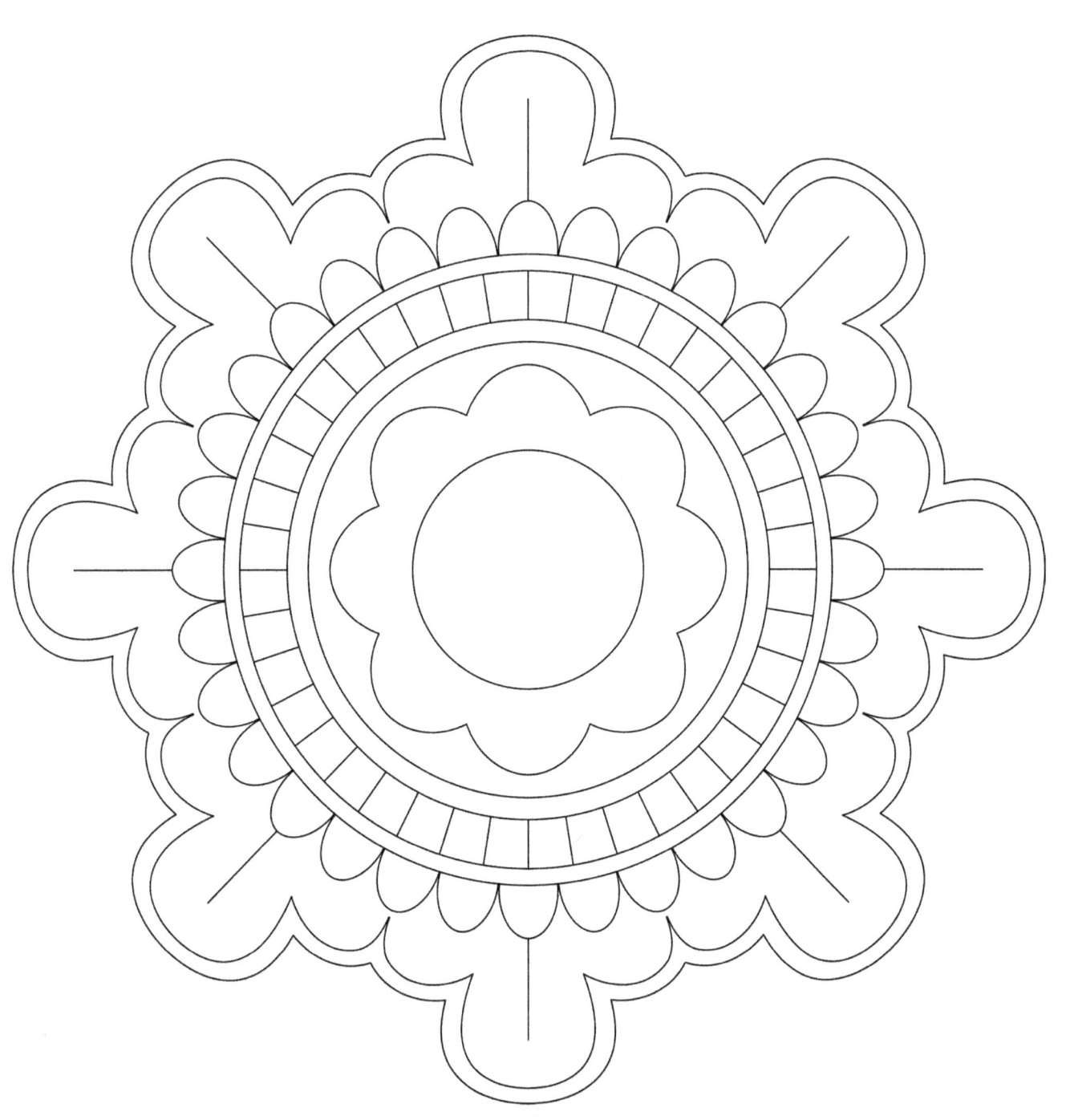

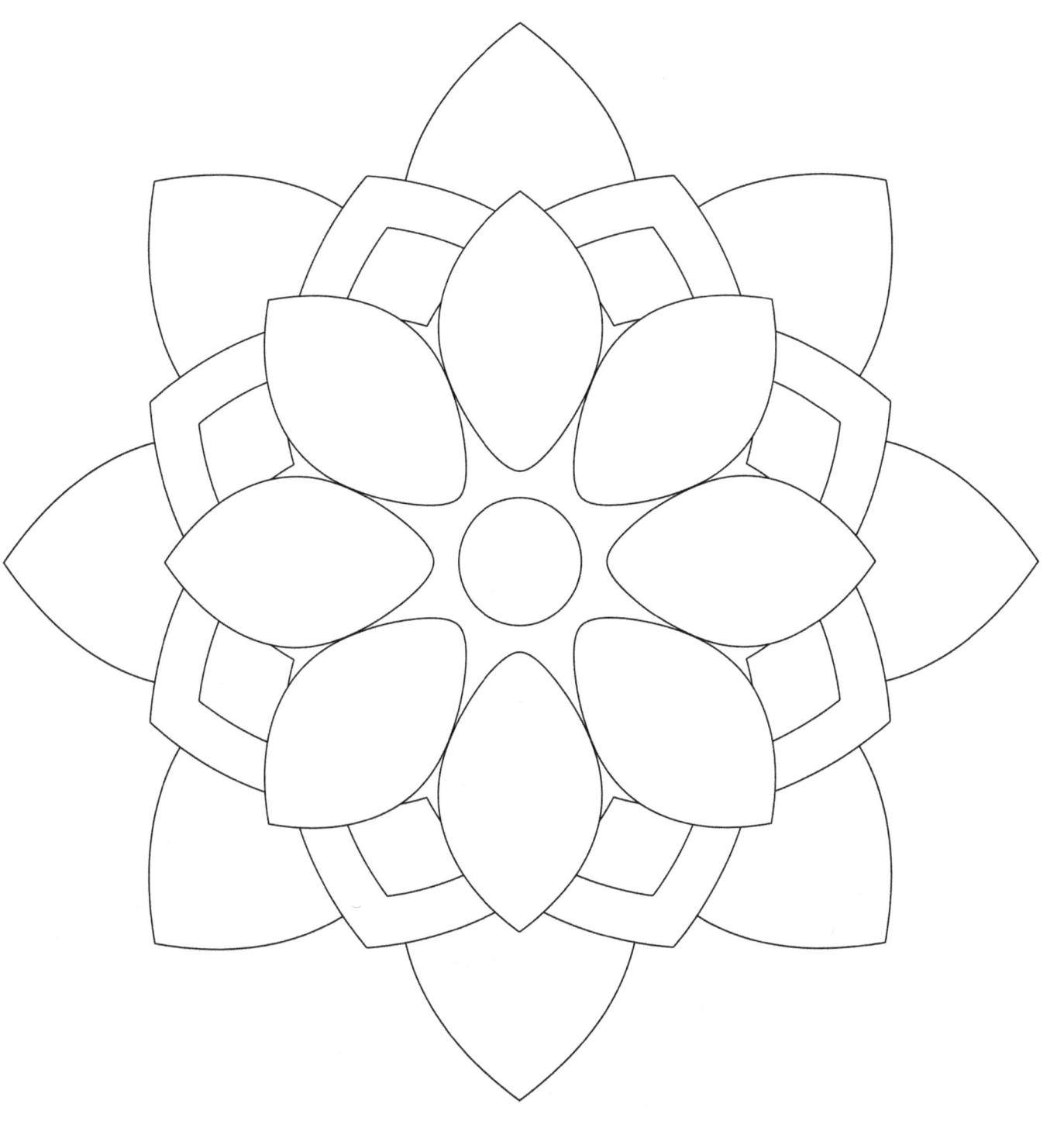

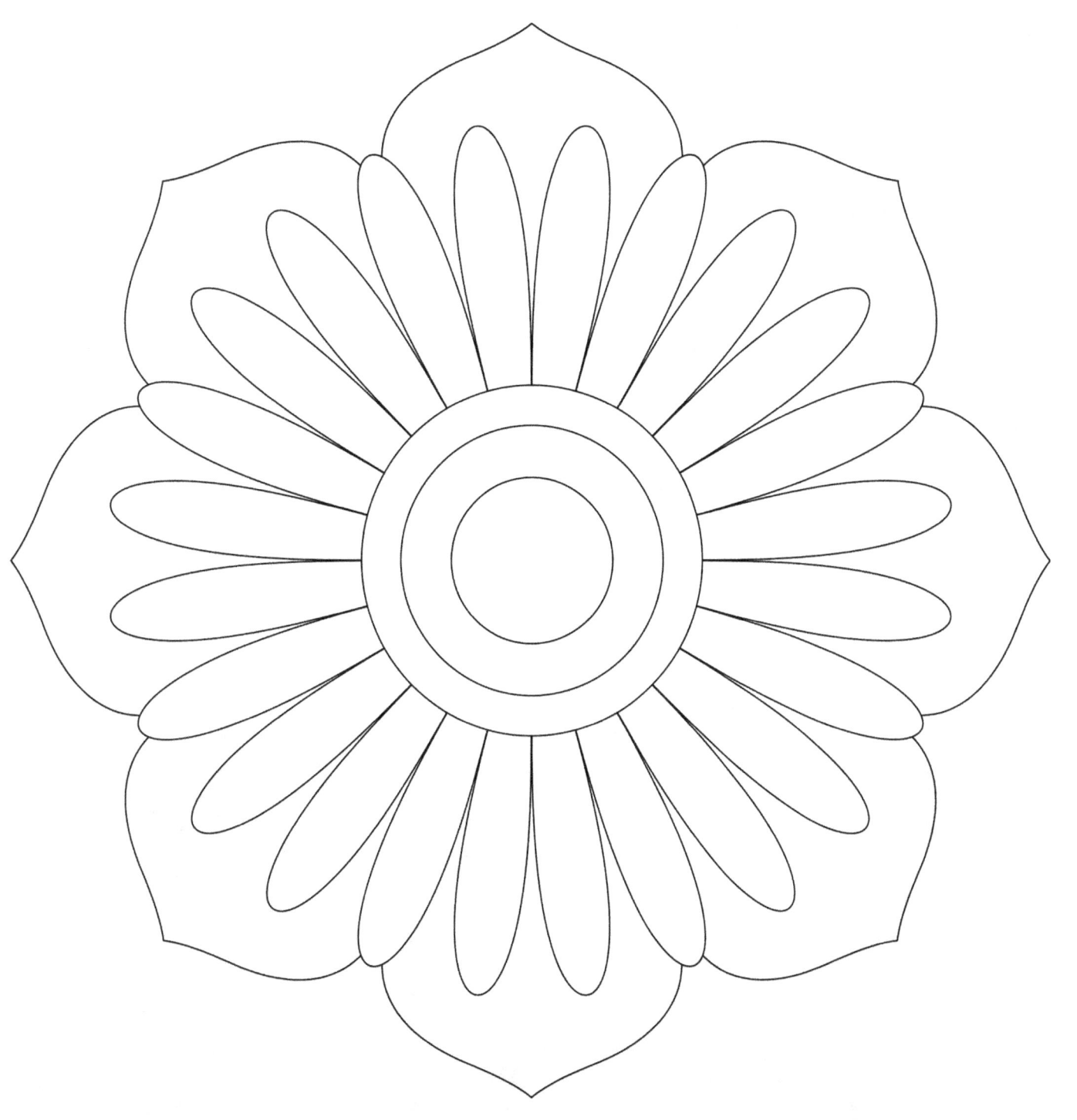

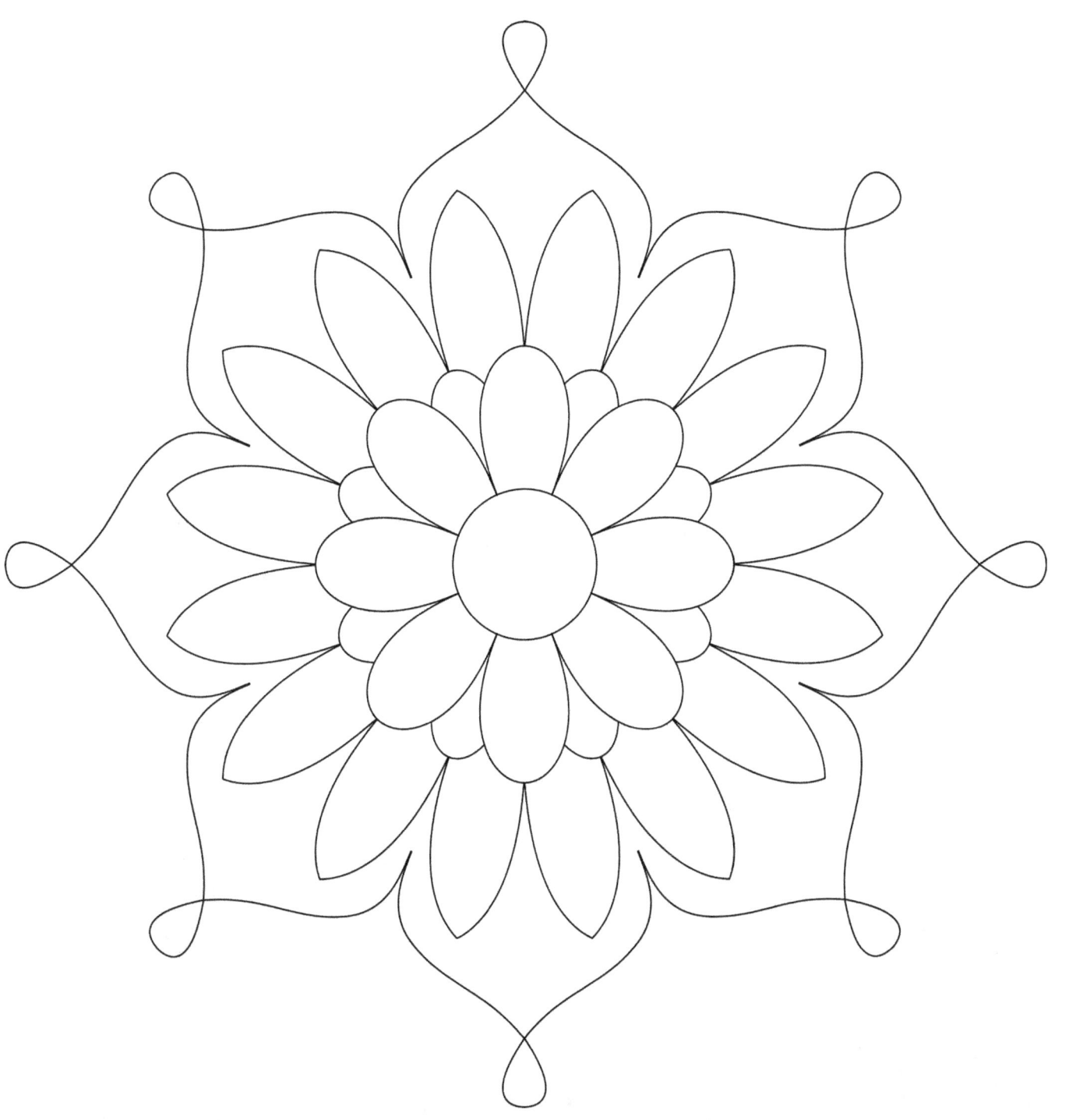

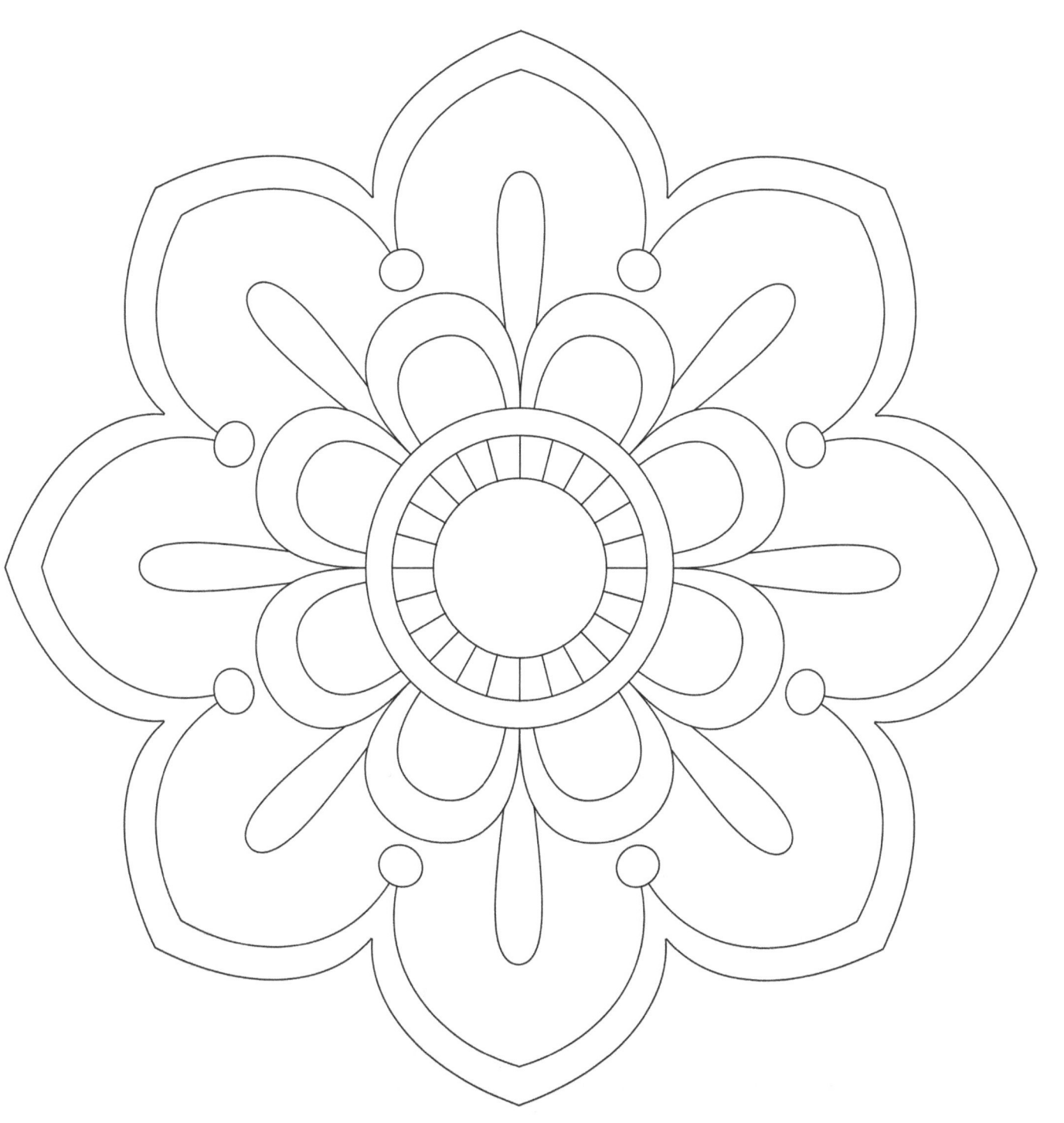

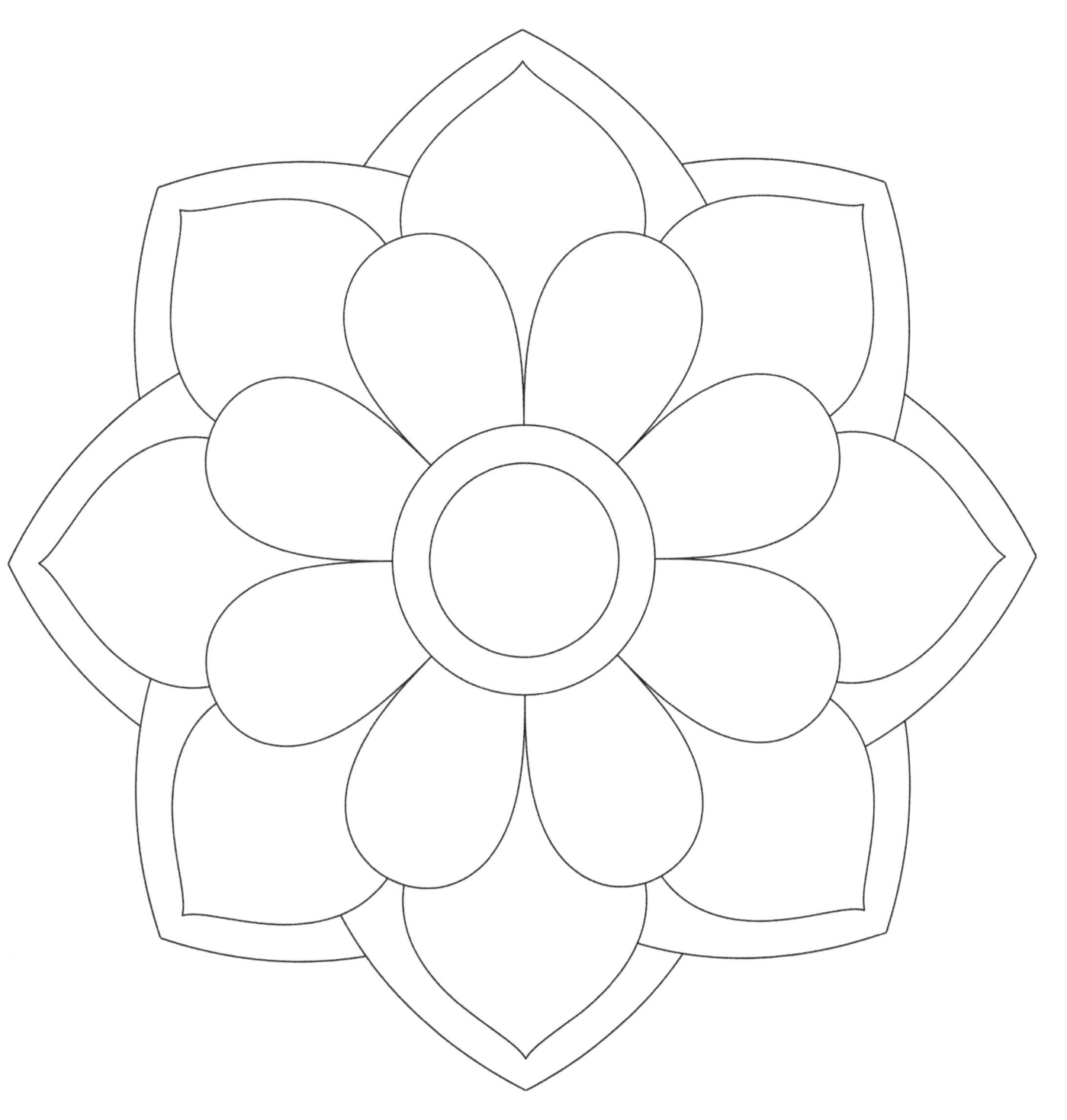

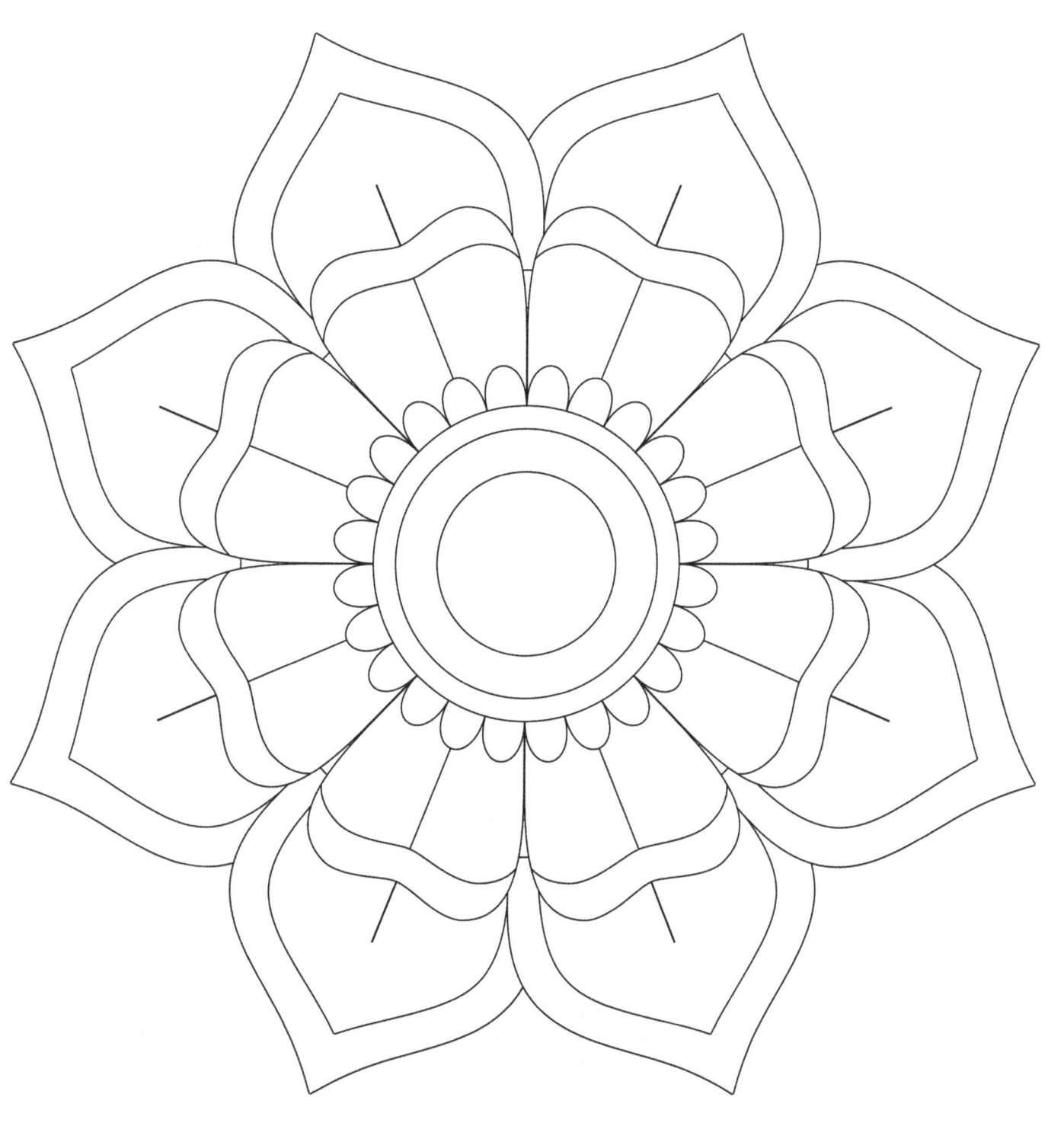

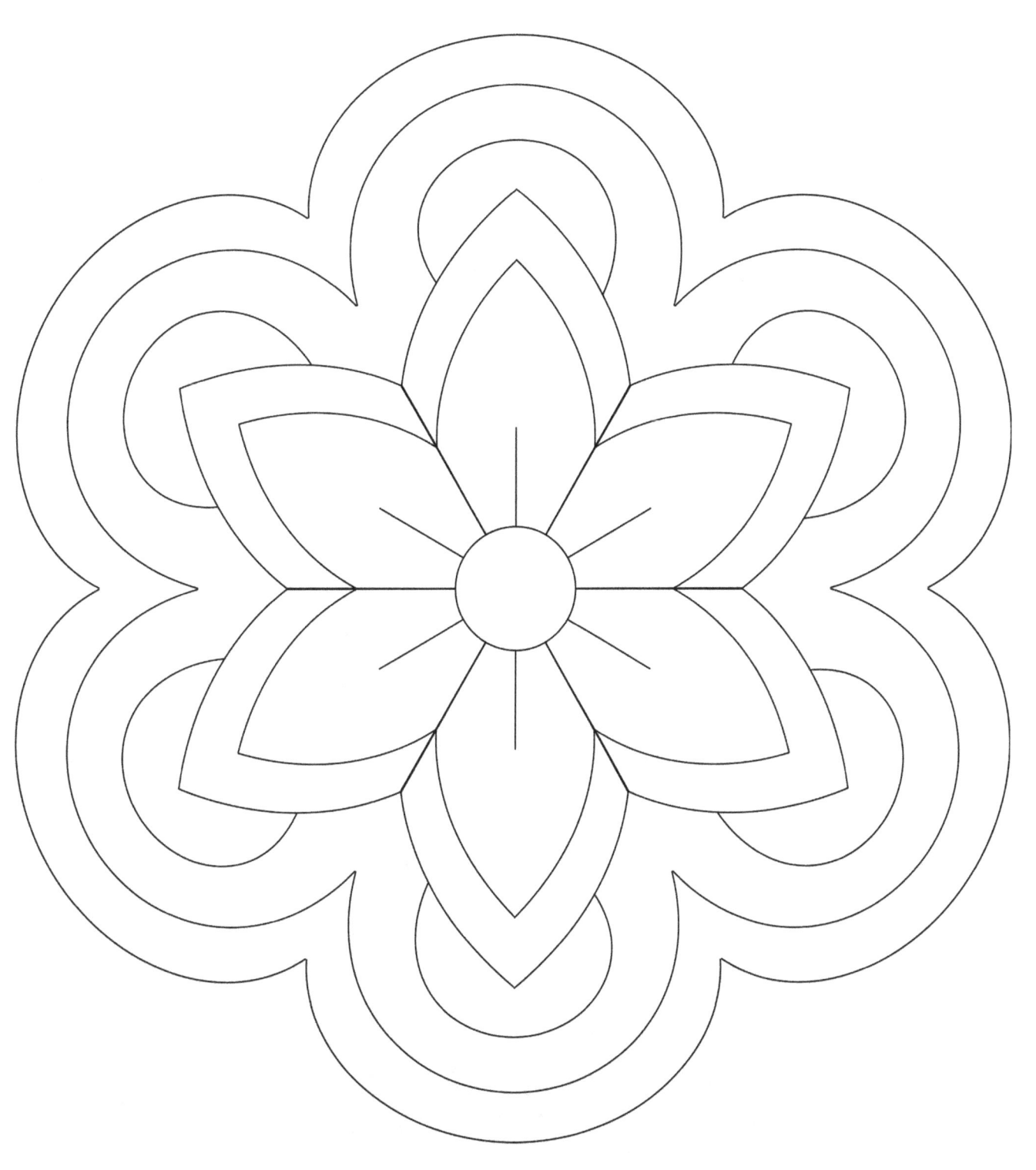

More From

selah Press.com

Devotionals | Journals | Coloring Books | Poetry
Family friendly books and journals to encourage and uplift.

Easy Coloring Books Series

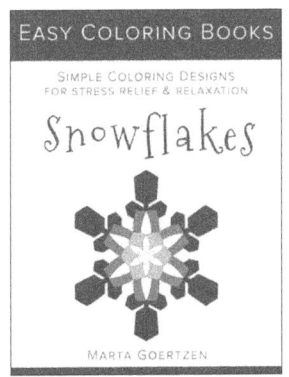

Daily Quiet Time Journals

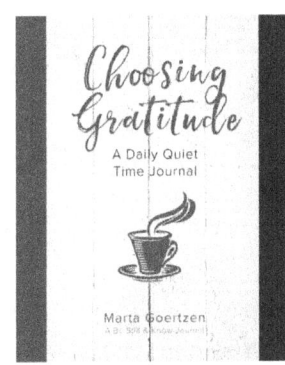
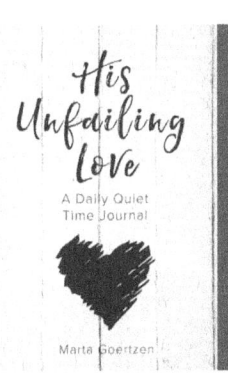

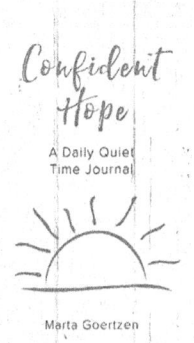